Francis Poulenc

Sonata
for oboe and piano

Revised edition, 2004

Edited by Millan Sachania

Includes audio demonstration and accompaniment tracks

CH83567

ISBN 978-1-78305-952-2

Edited and supervised by Sam Lung.
Oboe recorded by Christopher Cowie.
Piano recorded by Huw Watkins.
Audio mixed and mastered by Jonas Persson and Imogen Hall.
With special thanks to Dom Kelly and the English Session Orchestra.

Head office:
14–15, Berners Street,
London W1T 3LJ

Tel +44 (0)20 7612 7400
Fax +44 (0)20 7612 7549

Sales and hire:
Music Sales Distribution Centre,
Newmarket Road,
Bury St Edmunds,
Suffolk IP33 3YB

Tel +44 (0)1284 702600
Fax +44 (0)1284 768301

www.musicsalesclassical.com
e-mail: promotion@musicsales.co.uk

Chester Music

Francis Poulenc

SONATA FOR OBOE AND PIANO

Writing from the south of France in July 1962 to R. Douglas Gibson, the Managing Editor of J. & W. Chester, Francis Poulenc quipped that 'j'ai mis à mijoter, dans la même casserole, une sonate pour hautbois et celle pour clarinette' — *i.e.* that he was 'cooking' the oboe and clarinet sonatas in the same pan. The shared genesis of these two works is easily detected in the music: compare, for instance, bars 48–53 of the first movement of the oboe sonata with bars 78–83 of the first movement of the clarinet sonata. Though written in 1962, the two sonatas had been in Poulenc's thoughts for at least five years. The composer informed Gibson in 1957 that he had begun work on the bassoon sonata and that he envisioned two more woodwind sonatas, one for oboe and the other for clarinet. By February 1962, Poulenc's ideas had taken shape. In a letter to Pierre Bernac, he wrote that the two sonatas were 'très débrouillées', repeating this phrase in another letter to Bernac in August.[1] Although Poulenc dated the final manuscript of the oboe sonata 'Eté 1962', a letter to Bernac in November that year indicates that he was still tinkering with the final movement (which Poulenc considered 'une sorte de chant liturgique'). He sent the manuscript to Gibson in January 1963, asking that the engraving be entrusted to 'un bon graveur assez musicien pour deviner les notes douteuses'. A few days later, the composer suddenly died. The first edition was thus published posthumously, and, in spite of Poulenc's request to Gibson, it contained a number of errors and misreadings.

The objectives of this new edition are to reassess Poulenc's intentions, to correct errors and to refine and clarify the notation. Its underlying aim is to supply a score for performing musicians that is constructed along scholarly lines. The primary source is Poulenc's final manuscript, deposited at the Bibliothèque nationale, Paris [F-Pn: ms 23577]. In addition, I have consulted Poulenc's earlier draft [F-Pn: ms 23578], which also dates from the summer of 1962. Because the two sources differ in a number of respects, the few editorial decisions influenced by the draft are discussed below.

A comparison of the two sources discloses much about Poulenc's compositional process. Particularly fascinating are Poulenc's revisions to the dynamics — the oboe begins *mf*, not *pp*, in the draft, for instance — and the extent to which the later manuscript aerates the original textures by excising the oboe from certain bars (such as bar 29 in the first movement, where the oboe originally repeated the music of bar 28). Poulenc was pleased with the resulting textures and commended them to Bernac, observing that both the oboe and clarinet sonatas were 'très bien équilibré instrumentalement. Piano très clair.'

A few specific editorial points. First, the left-hand piano chord in bar 68 of the second movement reads d^1, gb^1, ab^1 in the later source, which seems erroneous. More implausible still is the combination d^1, g^1, ab^1 printed in the 1963 edition. I have thus plumped for the d^1, ab^1, bb^1 of the earlier source, which, together with the other notes sounding in this bar, provide for a B flat dominant thirteenth that resolves neatly to the E flats in the ensuing bar.

Also noteworthy is the reappearance of the music of bars 2–3 in bars 136–37 and 145–46 in the second movement. In the 1963 edition the later bars are identical to bars 2–3. This is not so in either source; the left-hand gb^1s of bar 2 and bar 3 are bb^1s in the later passages. Is the extra ledger line a slip? In spite of the resulting inconsistency between earlier and later passages, the present edition follows the sources. Not only is their notation here unequivocal, but Poulenc also uses a B♭, not a G, in the analogous bars 89 and 180. There is no question of a mix-up with the ledger lines here, since the B♭, now an octave lower than previously, is firmly attached to the bass-clef stave.

Poulenc's crescendo hairpins in the piano part of bars 8 and 13 of the third movement merit comment, since they are impossible to realise in the context of the sustained chords to which they apply. They are nevertheless worth preserving in print, since these dynamics convey to the pianist the musical direction of these bars — the effect that Poulenc would have liked had the piano been capable of achieving it.

A final remark on phrases that conclude with tied notes. Poulenc habitually ends the slur on the first of the tied notes, excluding the subsequent note or notes from the phrased unit. This is such a distinctive feature of Poulenc's notational style that I have decided to retain it.

MILLAN SACHANIA
Shepperton, England, 2004

---

[1] Relevant passages from Poulenc's letters to Bernac are quoted in Carl B. Schmidt, *The Music of Francis Poulenc* (Oxford, 1995), pp. 511–12.

à la mémoire de Serge Prokofieff

SONATA

for Oboe and Piano

FRANCIS POULENC

I

Elégie

*) Respecter soigneusement le doigté.

II
Scherzo

Francis Poulenc

Sonata
for oboe and piano

Revised edition, 2004

Edited by Millan Sachania
Includes audio demonstration and accompaniment tracks

Oboe part

Chester Music

SONATA

for Oboe and Piano

OBOE

FRANCIS POULENC

I

Elégie

4

II
Scherzo

III
Déploration

Selected works by
Francis Poulenc

1899–1963

Piano Solo
Album of Six Pieces
    Mouvements perpétuels No. 1
    Presto from Suite in C
    Impromptu No. 3
    Française
    Novelette No. 1
    Promenade No. 1 (A Pied)
Five Impromptus
Mouvements perpétuels
Three Novelettes
    No. 1 in C major
    No. 2 in B♭ minor
    No. 3 in E minor (on a theme of Manuel de Falla)
Ten Promenades
Suite in C

Piano Duets
Sonata (Prelude–Rustique–Final)
    (also suitable for two pianos, four hands)

Chamber Music
Elégie for horn and piano
Mouvements perpétuels
    orchestrated by the composer for 9 players (1946)
    arr. Heifetz, violin and piano
    arr. Levering, flute and guitar
    arr. Levering, 2 guitars
Sextet for piano, flute, oboe, clarinet, horn and bassoon
Sonata for flute and piano
Sonata for oboe and piano
Sonata for clarinet and piano
Sonata for two clarinets
Sonata for clarinet and bassoon
Sonata for horn, trumpet and trombone
    (also transcribed Nestor for flute and guitar)
Trio for oboe, bassoon and piano
Rapsodie nègre for low voice and two violins, viola,
    cello, flute, clarinet in B♭ and piano

CHESTER MUSIC

(a division of Music Sales Ltd)
14/15 Berners Street, London, W1T 3LJ
Exclusive Distributors: Music Sales Ltd
Newmarket Road, Bury St Edmunds, Suffolk, IP33 3YB

www.musicsalesclassical.com

Order No. CH83567

12

*) See Editorial Preface.

III
Déploration

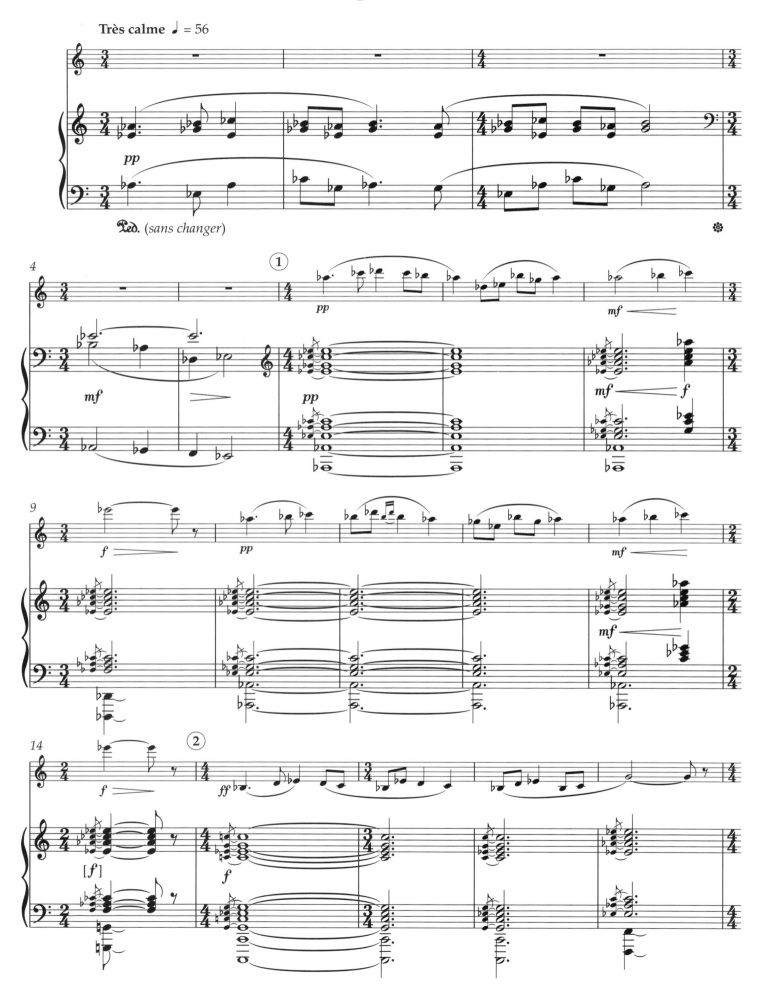

Brive – Bagnols-en-Forêt
Eté 1962

HOW TO DOWNLOAD YOUR MUSIC TRACKS

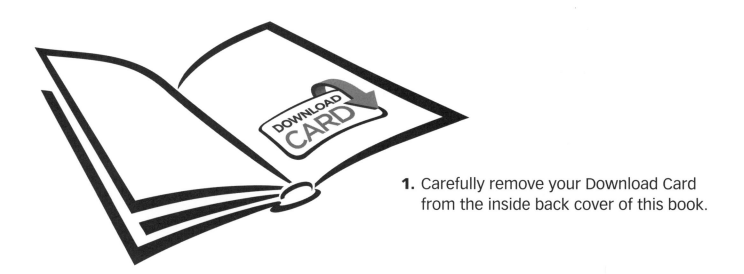

1. Carefully remove your Download Card from the inside back cover of this book.

TO REDEEM THIS CARD VISIT
www.musicsalesdownloads.com

ENTER ACCESS CODE:

XXXXXXXXXX

Download Cards are powered by Dropcards.
User must accept terms at dropcards.com/terms
which are adopted by The Music Sales Group.
Not reedemable for cash. Void where prohibited or restricted by law.

DCARD01006478

2. On the back of the card is your unique access code. Enter this at www.musicsalesdownloads.com

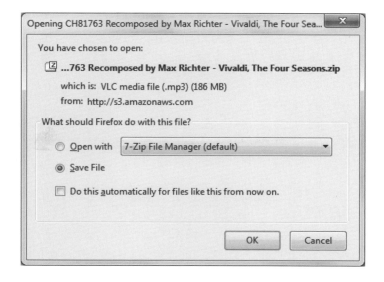

Opening CH81763 Recomposed by Max Richter - Vivaldi, The Four Sea...

You have chosen to open:

...763 Recomposed by Max Richter - Vivaldi, The Four Seasons.zip

which is: VLC media file (.mp3) (186 MB)

from: http://s3.amazonaws.com

What should Firefox do with this file?

○ Open with   7-Zip File Manager (default)

◉ Save File

☐ Do this automatically for files like this from now on.

OK   Cancel

3. Follow the instructions to save your files to your computer*. That's it!

*Appearance of download manager will vary depending upon operating system and web browser.
In case of difficulty when downloading files, please contact dropcards.com/help
Card missing? Please contact music@musicsales.co.uk